My e Book

by Jane Belk Moncure
illustrated by Vera Gohman

THE CHILD'S WORLD

ELGIN, ILLINOIS 60120

Library of Congress Cataloging in Publication Data

Moncure, Jane Belk.
  My "e" book.

  (My first steps to reading)
  Rev. ed. of: My "e" sound box. © 1984.
  Summary: Little "e" fills his box with eggs, elves,
and other things beginning with the short letter "e."
  1. Children's stories, American. [1. Alphabet]
I. Gohman, Vera Kennedy, 1922-   ill.   II. Moncure,
Jane Belk.   My "e" sound box.   III. Title.
IV. Series: Moncure, Jane Belk.   My first steps to
reading.
PZ7.M739Mye 1984b   [E]   84-17545
ISBN 0-89565-273-0

Distributed by Childrens Press, 1224 West Van Buren Street,
Chicago, Illinois 60607.

My "e" Book

(This book concentrates on the short "e" sound in the story line. Words beginning with the long "e" sound are included at the end of the book.)

Little  had a **box**.

"I will fill my **box**," he said.

Little found eggs,

eggs, eggs.

8

He put the eggs
into his box.

Little e found elves.

10

The elves danced
and danced.

Then Little  put the elves into his box.

The elves played with
the eggs.

"Be careful, elves,"

said Little .

Now the box was heavy.

So Little  found an elephant, a big elephant.

"Hop on," said the elephant.

The elephant went up and down.

The eggs fell out of the box.

The elves fell too.

So did Little e.

19

"What a mess," Little e said.

"Now who will help me fill my box?"

box

An Eskimo came by.

"I will help you," he said.

box

box

"We will find lots of eggs."

Guess where he found eggs for Little ?

Guess who had pretty eggs for everyone?

elephant

box

elves

26

eggs

Eskimo

27

More words with Little

elevator

envelope

Little  has another sound in some words.

He says his name.

Listen for Little e's name.

eagle

eel

emu

Easter